AF244797

Left at the Ruin

Also by Jacqueline Berger

The Day You Miss Your Exit
The Gift that Arrives Broken
Things that Burn
The Mythologies of Danger

Left at the Ruin

Jacqueline Berger

Terrapin Books

Terrapin Books
4 Midvale Avenue
West Caldwell, NJ 07006

www.terrapinbooks.com

ISBN: 978-1-947896-76-5
Library of Congress Control Number: 2024939008

First Edition

Cover art: by Judith Greenwald
Fresh, 2008, 30" x 22"
combined media / acrylic

Cover design: Diane Lockward

for Jeff

Contents

Four

Five

One

Blade

Walking down the back stairs to my office,
I like to look through my neighbor's window
to see the three knives that appear to be
sticking out of the wall as though thrown.
Sometimes my neighbor's at her table
and I quickly turn away.
I've moved the large white chair
to the center of my room so I can see the garden,
French doors open if the weather is fine,
the weeping trees, their blossoms
dangling like tassels.
Now the neighbor's lean cat,
tortoiseshell coat shiny in the sun,
wanders through, leisurely looking
for something to kill.
A wall is a good place for a knife,
the handle at arm's reach, the blade
partially tucked into the wood
like a story you live with
but don't need to always talk about.

Only Goodnight

We did not marry awestruck, riled.
We were forty and both
blown off course by passion
more than once and came back
limping on a makeshift cane.
We wanted solid. And we were afraid,
I was, to be alone. Women my age
had a better chance of being hit
by lightning than marrying.
Who funded that study?
August wedding on a hillside.
I wore a boned bodice
embroidered cream and rose.
I wouldn't let myself imagine
more than five years out.
Now it is almost twenty.

My single self tells a friend
love was the house,
but desire the dog
whining to be let in, let out.
My married self says we learned
to let what howls, howl
and what loves, love.

Should I have left?
I put the question
in a past I can't return to.

Every night I curl myself
into your lap before bed—
night owl husband, hours
before you join me—
and we stay curled sometimes
as though we were saying goodbye
instead of only goodnight.

Forecast

Maybe it's Saturn
returning after a slow orbit
of the sun to its natal
position on my chart
that's throwing cosmic dust
like grit in the gears.
Or maybe it's the seven
years since my parents left me
free-falling through the geometry of space
where looking out is looking back
in the loop and bend of time.
Or the countdown of my own columns,
the ache in my left thumb,
click in my knee
that's making me restless
as wind trapped in a courtyard.
Without canyons to howl down
or trees to frenzy,
it swirls wrappers, plasters
yesterday's paper to a fence.
A plastic bag sails by,
its clear body for a minute
airborne as a spirit.

Bitter

Children like sweet
and salt. The adult mouth
craves the peculiar
pleasures of olives, quinine,
espresso with a peel of lemon,
a Manhattan or Old Fashioned—
dash of bitters,
cardamom, coriander, momentary
sting that warms.

Bitter melon, bitter chocolate.
The imagination as well
acquires a taste for pepper
added to cake, horseradish
to cream, grudges
like copper pots
gleaming on the range.

Not the Wolf but the Dog

Not the zebra but the horse,
not buffalo but cows,
maybe camels,
who abandoned the wild for the stable,
a stall lined in straw,
wee gables and eaves,
their name over the door—
Biscuit, Coco. Snowball, Ranger.
Who traded the hunt
for the daily bowl and dish,
predators for owners, collar and leash;
agreed to be a tool—plow or cart
or confidant—to breed in captivity.

So when the man in the elevator
at the Venetian holding his cardboard
tray of coffees and muffins
heading back to his room
says to no one in particular,
but most likely to the other man,
the three of us strangers,
I better get something in return for this,
"this" means fetching breakfast
so his wife can sleep,
I better get something for all of this,
gesturing with his head,
meaning the hotel, the dinners and shows,

when the man says this,
I think about women
in staggering heels, breasts like missiles,
who'd rather be feral than kept,
and about men who gave up wilding
to claim their offspring.

I'm carrying my own tray
of coffees and muffins,
will soon press the card against the lock,
open the room, rip off my clothes,
throw back the three hundred
thread count sheets, waking
my husband. He's met someone new
and now wants both
of his lives at once.
He can sleep later. These untamed
weeks, we're savaging,
flesh against flesh, ravishing
our marriage.

But soon the holidays will be over
and we'll fly home, his Christmas gifts,
back when he thought he knew
what he wanted,
waiting to be put away,
the meat injector —
what brine does to the bird —
downloadable eBook included,
and the wooden mallet ice crusher

with its own canvas bag
for making Moscow mules
in their frosted copper mugs.

The dog took what the wolf
refused and became Pekinese,
French Bull, but still needs
to be trained to heel and sit.
And still sometimes runs
when the door's left open and needs
to be shouted at to come home.

Rosy Fingered Dawn

English-major humor,
Dawn on her back or knees,
Rosy's tapered fingers
entering.

Baffling, how time bends,
forty years since the girls
who taught me
girls could masturbate—
I'd only ever seen boys
miming it, a hand pulling a cord
to make a bell ring.

A cucumber, no, zucchini,
and after, returned
to the crisper. Mom
slicing that night for salad.
Gales of laughter. How often
we were a little hysterical
back then. Now
one of us wears a cancer scarf,
the others, big hats
in solidarity.
Forty years like wisps.
Do you remember—?

One does or doesn't
in the gust and flurry,

our little boats bobbing.
Little boats lifting
and slamming.
Still, dawn comes early,
her arms laden with roses.

The History of What Never Happened

What never happened never happened
if never spoken of,
never lifted from the cave
and carried blinking into daylight.
We held our breath
passing the cemetery,
family drive after dinner for soft serve
dipped in chocolate, the wonder
of swirls not toppling into the vat,
and held our breath on the way back,
cones in hand, gently melting.
What did we learn from listening
to what our parents never said?

Let the children skip across graves,
another place to play.
Windy April bursts the pods and powders skin,
and someone starts to dance
and soon the fields of the dead are full
of swirling skirts puffed wide as bells.

Loophole

The origin is a narrow aperture,
arrow slit or loop
that's come to mean an opening
in any structure, be it castle
or marriage. So when my lover
spits on his finger to wet
what is wet already,
and holds my hand,
plowing his beauty,
its foreign power, into me,
and when the hatch at the center
of my heart flies open,
I am unhinged,
and you, inches away
are watching.
Fidelity's loophole.
You have never seen me so
ecstatic and love me
more for what you see.

On our sofa I pull the throw
over myself and you under join me
in the small dark,
animals in a tunnel of wet leaves.

We are ourselves again,
the festival of madness behind us.

Though I still *pine*, your word,
for the one I barely know and now
it seems can't live without.

Give desire a boundary
and it sails across.
Marry it and see how quiet
and still, growing downward
in deep soil. We have
no idea how to live. Our last
decade before the work
of age begins in earnest.

First Kiss

Rag of memory pulled from the dirty basket—
temple youth group, kibbutz
close enough to the border
we could hear the Arab market.
A wedding that night, streamers,
lights in the trees.
I hadn't been drinking but others
must have been. A soldier
I'd seen at the pool—
one was different than the rest, tenderhearted,
that was not the one who liked me—
took my hand and led me to his room.
Our parents had paid to have us *experience*,
all summer that word.
A quick look around before
he turned out the light.
Full dark. The darkest part of dark.
Then we were on the bed,
was there anywhere else to sit?
His mouth on mine, and quick,
his finger inside me—was it
his finger? Maybe two. I couldn't tell
and was very still
trying to know.
Go ahead and ask
why I stayed, ask
if any part of me wanted.

I stayed because I couldn't
figure out how to leave. How long
before I remembered
one leaves by standing up and walking
to the door unless one is prevented
first by words and then by hands.
But no, in this story he didn't prevent.
I wonder now if my soldier—
can I claim him,
pin him to the flannel of memory?—
wonder if he'd killed,
and if he had killed if all he could do
was drown his fingers
in the never-been-touched lake of me.
Perhaps he would be dead by twenty.
I walked back to the wedding party,
streamers and lights like eyes in the trees.
Or the party was over and I found
my way back to the dorm in the dark.

Elsewhere

Though I can appreciate the physics,
the complex system of pulleys,
I would never want to be pierced
by hooks and dangled
from the tented skin
of my back or thighs,
suspended in air.
The young man in the video—
bookish, sweet—his voice-over
narrates the route,
boring, nothing to look at but misty
Eastern European fields,
then another train through a city
grey with rain, and up the stairs
to the apartment of a woman
covered in tattoos, but motherly
in a flowered dress,
tying the special knots on what
looks like a circular loom.

Ancient ritual of penance
or devotion I want for some reason
to watch. The boy does not tell
the story of his damage, but what else
would encourage him
to hang by the skin of his own body?

Now he wipes his palms on his jeans,
undresses and lies on the floor
while the woman slips on latex gloves,
infection the bigger danger than tearing,
the body's leather surprisingly tough.
Then the hooks are through,
no more than a thin line of blood.
I want to see how far he will go.
Is this the reason
I can't stop watching?
He doesn't scream
but goes silent,
his voice replaced by music.
Now he is hoisted
several feet above ground,
and the woman gently spins him.
Later he will tell us how the pain, unlike
any he's experienced before,
turned trance-like as he drifted
into elsewhere.
It unravels you—
he's speaking directly
to the camera now that it's over—
opens every emotional valve.

In the end, the woman gathers
the boy in her arms as a parent
after punishment might do.
He shuts his eyes as she rocks him,
his face smooth and still in her hands.

Women with Men

Walking one evening
with my husband in the park,
we hear a man moaning from the bathroom—
a girl on her knees
clutching the toilet,
the guy taking her from behind.
Should we call the police?
Or yell to see if she needs help?
According to my husband,
they're just kids too drunk
to care about the public
setting of their sex.
True, we didn't see her struggle.
Do nothing, keep walking,
the cinderblocks darkening behind us.

A dozen years ago
but I think of her sometimes.
Girl on her knees,
now nearing thirty,
does she remember
that night, or is it lost
in a blur of bad
or semi-bad, or only messy
attempts at love?
Maybe she was dragged
from the path

and what looked like lack
of struggle was betrayal,
her voice on mute and her body,
what could she do but abandon it?
My own voice
buried like a small animal
under a tree another animal
digs up and devours.

Two

Telling

I peed in a chair last night.
Walked right by the restroom
on my way to the podium—
I'm going to read a selection
from my recently published—
detoured into the kindergarten,
stuffed myself into a wee chair, and wet.

I like to be hit over the head
by my dreamer, night poet
who encourages me
to tell you about the time
in the mountain diner
I laughed so hard I burst
and left a pool under the table,
which made us—old friends, an ex—
laugh harder, and I sailed my soiled pants,
light cotton, it was summer,
out the window to dry as we drove.

In my nice black skirt and boots,
adjusting the mic:
We are born not only naked but wet.
Smattering of applause, and now
you can go back to your own life
which is waiting, if you're lucky,

to expose you, as mine does,
pant legs wide as wind sleeves
in the August air.

Method

Write down every thought
as it arises, develops, passes
its baton to the next
without fabrication or hypocrisy
for three days after which—Freud
quoting a minor German Romantic—
you will be a writer.
Does the pencil change
the mind's meandering,
forcing focus, *fabricating*?
Capture the calculus of association,
enter the art house
or Cineplex of thought—
if auteur then brooding,
if big budget then garish emotionality's
grand explosions, bodies
summersaulting through air.
Be a flaneur passing windows
and winter trees.
Include the hours when the inner talker
is a bureaucrat at a metal desk
tallying the petty complaints of a day.
Notice how often you repeat yourself.
Believe you are finally admitting what's true.

Circus

A woman bends over
her ledger, desire to one side,
despair to the other,
the sides of her palms
ink stained dark as paws.
Men should audition for sex,
offering the tender underside
of their necks, heads thrown back,
as the sword swallower, a comely man
in a vintage suit, is doing right now
before sending one blade
after another down his throat,
then five at once, a bouquet of swords—
he is not afraid to commit.

The opposite of swallowing—
relax the sphincter of the esophagus
to turn the ring of muscles
into a living scabbard.
A boy spends hours practicing,
avoiding whatever is exploding
on the other side of his bedroom door.
What does a girl practice?

Another night of mad accounting
for her, another near miss, lungs
and stomach recoiling in terror

for him. What we do for love.
The day the circus ends,
the big top's hoisted sky
unstaked, collapsed,
its dirty canvas roped and bound
until the show begins again.

The Wolf Indicator

A good man avoids
the no-fly zone
of a daughter's body.
That leaves arms and hair
and feet and back and shoulders and knees
and calves and ankles.
He's been dead a decade
and I still can't put into words—
can't or won't—
but today the new hygienist,
young, gay, fresh from training,
really wants to talk
about my teeth.
So now I'm telling
the story of the fang.
Thirteen when it arrived,
its brief reign
between appearance and correction.
A latent fierceness
otherwise unexpressed,
how I continue the story
to myself on the train.
Eighteen when I finally told
my father to stop.
Though really, the problem
was I was a girl
who couldn't stand to be touched,

it seems I was like that
even as a baby.
I don't remember
which tooth was the fang,
though I do remember headgear, the ache
when the orthodontist deepened
the pressure with hooks and bands.
Look, I showed the hygienist,
I still have my wisdom teeth.
Which is something not many can say.

Beggar

What a waste when I was young not loving
but obsessing over imaginary, unavailable.
Not for me, the prelude of hands
brushing against each other passing sugar.
Nor chapter one, the unbuttoning,
shirts like spilled cream on the worn floor;
chapters two through five,
a fight, a change of scenery, a feast,
the cleanup left for morning
as the lovers retreat to the nest
at the top of the stairs
the summer they live in the old sea house.
Roommates fail to see the charm
of lobster shells and half-eaten chocolates,
soiled napkins like wilted peonies and the faint
sound of laughter leaking through the ceiling.
Not mine, the final chapter where the hero
bicycles through the winter landscape,
ash and bone, bare trees, a lone figure
on a path through the woods.
My heart was a tin cup
rattling its single coin like a beggar
on the corner as the lovers passed,
one's hand tucked in the other's back pocket,
the whole sky laying down for them its silver.

Superpower

Turns out, most women want to disappear.
Forget flying—mythic, heroic,
swooping down to save the weak from the cruel—
we'd rather be invisible, get away
with shoplifting, watching sex, walking all night,
slipping the leash of safety, its endless warnings against.
What we want is to stop having skin,
fabric fed from a spool and spread
across a table to be stamped with pattern.
We prefer to be air,
the one thing no one can claim
and no one can live without.

Three

Beginning with H

I've always loved hover,
hoist, and heave —
what I did with a stick,
as though it were heavy,
into the waves for the dog,
not mine but the stranger's.
We picked him up
on the coast highway.
Newly licensed, now
we could drive ourselves,
but we still didn't know where to go.
You followed him into a cave.
Were you counting on me to come too?
Too late to say no
when I refused. But I wasn't
the one he wanted.

A girl saves herself
from force by conceding.
You came out, then he did,
I didn't ask what happened.
My hand on the stick
had found a nail and bled.
We hoarded ourselves, hid from,
best friends who haven't
seen each other since.

The Idea of a Useable Past

From the balcony
at the back of the house—
there is no view from nowhere;
we all stand somewhere—
fields the color of straw
and the old loves carving
jagged paths as they cross.
You recognize each
by their walk, loves you mostly
studied from a distance,
and recognize your own halt
and catch as you pass.

The debased historian
on the shaded portico—
you can't remember
what you can't remember—
a cold drink, a light sweater,
mining the past for insight.

Of the moral sense
to be pulled—
in a footnote, see Flattery.
Of evidence, as though
your life were on trial,
diagram a day.

Little cloud of insects as you cross.
Is white cotton see-through in sunlight?

An interpretive practice, looking back—
this moment too is passing, past—
though further inquiry
those who seriously
consider the subject
agree is always needed.

Conjoined

Let me start by saying they're cute,
which always matters,
blond bob on one, long hair
on her twin, both of them cat-eyed,
the one who looks forward,
the one whose face is off to the side,
tilted as though in surprise.
From a distance, they look
like a two-headed person,
though there's no such thing.
What appears as a single body
actually has two hearts,
two stomachs, three lungs.
How many vaginas?
someone posts, though
that's not covered in the video
where the girls are talking
about how much they love clothes
and football games, cider after
with their friends, and their new job
as a teacher, teachers, in a third-grade class.
In the 70s two performance artists
tied themselves together
for a year to test their limits.
Did they ever cheat and untie
in desperation? Something,
of course, the twins can't do.

They want to marry, have children.
Hence the question about their parts.
If they ever feel like circus freaks—
they hate when strangers take their picture,
that's as close as they come to admitting
what it's like, though their compatriots
in history rode on caravans
and carnies barked their horrible wonder.
On the family sofa, these two
couldn't be more wholesome;
still, I'm lured and can't stop watching,
though my husband walking by
sees what I'm up to and shakes his head.
Sometimes I talk to myself—who hasn't
consulted an invisible twin?—
though usually the conversation goes
something like, Jackie, what do you think
will happen? Jackie, I wish I knew.

Ten-Foot Chair in a Field of Weeds

Field already slated for condos and lofts—
the brief life of the giant chair
redefines the space as art
before it turns itself over to money.

I part the weeds, climb the ladder,
lean against the chair's enormous back.
Great view of abandoned boxcars,
the ribboned freeways, traffic bad,
the sky pale and worn.

Nothing belongs, or everything does
in the rusted beauty
that fanciness has not yet found,
in the silence of the blaring world,
world my mother is still a part of,
though soon, sooner than I imagine,
she will leave it.

Field I will never return to, field
that will be a field
for only a short time longer.

The Feeling of Will-Be-Over

Finally, I believe I will die.
The feeling arrives
like the smell of eucalyptus,
a medicine-cabinet smell.
Or is it more the sour of old ice
from the encrusted freezer's snow cove
back when bowls of hot water melted walls.
Or tar, or turpentine
in coffee tins, after-school oil painting,
little studio off Pico,
every Wednesday for years,
the rag dipped then rubbed on hands
to remove cadmium or cobalt
from the stand of trees
I'd rendered valiantly
if naively all afternoon.

I am grateful for nothing,
what I know of it,
the studio long gone,
my teacher dead, my mother as well,
and the Pinto she picked me up in
famously recalled for bursting
into flames on impact.

County

Today my students are writing poems
about food, an assignment they hate:
It makes us hungry. But they do
what seems to me their best work.
If they're listening, as I am, to your son's
happy shrieks through the wall—
you and your boy in the visitor's room,
first time you've seen him in months—
no one mentions it,
though most of them are mothers as well.
One woman writes of French toast,
butter melting beneath the knife
the year she was safe
living with her grandmother.
Another writes a list of bacons:
maple, hickory, pork, turkey;
gumbo appears in three different poems,
and buttered rice, grits, hot-water cornbread,
the sorrow of crawfish, oysters, melancholy
of sausage, pozole, the tender road back
of corn on the cob, someone gestures eating it,
and the true indignity of granola bars,
not the chewy kind but the dry
that the county provides for snacks.
I'm supposed to hand them out
so everyone gets just one.
They can fill their own plastic cups with water.

Tabasco, okra, shrimp—
by the end of the poem, the mother
not high in her room in the dark,
not turning out a daughter for dope,
the mother in a kitchen thick with steam—
drippings, crabmeat, filé powder, roux.

Looking for Hopper

Burgundy sofa, and her dress
a shade darker.
No, not sofa, so office, analyst's,
with the adjacent chair
becomes motel,
how could I have missed the valise,
two, little tags dangling off the handles.

The woman on the edge
of the bed is very straight.
Leaving or arriving?
And the man, though she is alone
in the painting, is he behind
the hard set of her mouth and eyes?
Undershade of sorrow —
how else know a stranger
than imagine myself in her?

Is that his car out the window,
green as the cube of light falling
over the walls and carpet?
Beyond — dry hills, cloudless sky,
a quarter moon,
no, only the ceiling fixture,
a daub of white.
She isn't showing —
but why complicate the simple

fact of an ample bosom
in a sleeveless dress,
her legs bare as well.

Evening and the heat
is finally beginning to break.

I Wake at 2 AM to a Girl

She and her friends, but her voice
rising above the rest, wake me, laughing.
Happy, or drunk, and from the displacement
of dream it's me in the street so late, so early,
my life has barely begun.

I hold a grudge against myself,
the missing bounty of my thoughtless years,
the sheer joy of being a body,
keeping it up all night, why did I think
I needed so much sleep?
My deathbed self will likely
look back with similar regret on me.

The girls have moved on, buoyant, sloppy,
holding each other to steady.
When I wake again, it's morning,
and my heart is heavy as an heirloom
lugged from place to place.

Dear Future, I begin the letter
I've been meaning to write,
Do you call yourself old at 80?
Are you still alive, still tending
the storeroom of memory?
Distance flattens the contours,
so let me remind you

that nothing was simple,
why it took me so long
to decide about Jeff, why
I didn't have an affair with A.

Girl forty years behind me,
your future will forget
this morning's pounding head
and sour stomach, recall only,
as it should, the reckless
entitlement of joy.

Offseason

The Anchor is open all winter.
Half the town are drunks,

the other half collect
medallions at meetings.

By February, they'll switch places.
We are lying under a lake of stars

waiting for our lives to begin.
By spring what's bramble

will be blackberries.
And the future, a ride that arrives

before we are ready to leave.

Assertion

Once I washed a stranger's face
and stared into his eyes.
We were learning how to sit
with the dying.
The plague years.
Young men walking
with canes in our city,
skeletal, bruised.

The opposite of assertion,
to be seen unarranged.
I will stare into your catastrophe
and let you stare into mine.
He worked for the opera,
the stranger before me,
your face without makeup,
he said, *how beautiful.*
That's what seemed to surprise him.

The Door of Mercy

A woman leaps from her seat
and bounds into the aisle,
swaying and clapping her hands over her head
to the Sephardic renditions,
oud and mandolin,
of the melodies we grew up with,
her face shiny with joy.
Not young or lithe
like girls at concerts who stand
on their seats to dance, shirts lifted
to show the flat stones of their stomachs,
the woman in the aisle
is wearing a houndstooth dress,
a little tight through the middle,
each tooth the size of a fist.
My own fountain of joy
is not spilling over,
as evidenced by my writing
this dark note on the back of the insert
in the prayer book, my hand
the only moving part of me.
What would it take to give
myself over to the holy?
I am bent not in prayer but judgment,
scribbling my small thoughts,
or not small, if I could reach down
to the core, the shame or anger

that keeps me from throwing open
the window of my life to breathe.
The woman in the aisle is not thinking
of how she appears, or if she is,
a larger, freer part lifts her high above,
Who do you think you are?
Maybe it has taken her whole life
to arrive here.
If she had a tambourine
she would be shaking it.
And when God opens the door
of mercy on this day of awe,
she is already halfway through.

Left at the Ruin

Smashed apricots on the stone road,
a few still on the branches.
I am writing to remember
how to get back to my hotel
through the maze of streets.
Walking slowly, stopping often
to record in a little notebook
another landmark.

This coming to yourself,
what is it?
Poetry final, two hours,
our teacher only half joking.

Forty years ago,
and I still don't know how to answer.

Frying onion, aubergine,
is scent a landmark?
Is sound?
The breakfast dishes and silver,
a woman's voice, then a cry —
child or cat? Town of strays
sleeping in the shade.

Pay attention
is as close as I get.

But how often must I pass
before the mind claims what the eye
must surely each time see?
Pink elephant on the poster,
martini in its trunk.
Then the ubiquitous erection,
purple, on a passage wall—
thank you young scrawler,
your anxious expression of power,
for the marker. And thank you
to the young woman in the dress shop,
bored, waiting it seems
for her life to begin.
And to old women, bowlegged, in black.
The shuffle of their slippers on stone.
These vertical streets.

A final is never final.
I am still afraid of myself
though less so.

Now I have almost made it back.
Left at the ruin,
its open wound of plaster and rust,
then right at the hotel's old gate,
open, it seems as though
it hasn't shut in years.

Four

Food Is Not Medicine

I should know to eat beforehand
when she asks me to lunch,
just hot water for her.
Call food medicine, as she does,
and we're only feeding the animal
of the body so it can work.
Weighing and measuring,
intermittent fasting, swallowing
dinner in pill form—so many
versions of the leash.

It's true, desire is endless
and legendary, her battle
with narrow-hipped discipline,
but make medicine
out of longing and lose butter—
the mouth consents
to being coated, greased
to the roof, consents
to baked goods
flavoring the walls of the cave,
trace of sugar
and flour on the lips,
little puffs like breath in winter,
wreaths floating in air.

If medicine, then lost
is the lamb and the boar

along with the bonfire,
the children past their bedtimes,
faces bright from flames,
hair smelling of roasted meat,
learning through fireside stories
and songs how to be.
Lost, the white cloth and candles,
the solitary meal celebrating itself,
a little forced, okay,
or the shared, eating as prelude,
pleasure leading to pleasure,
a small bouquet of posies
blossoming briefly in their water.

Medusa

Did she befriend
her snakes? Unexpected
gift of hideous—ugly
is a loaded gun.

Livid, tangled,
did the vipers tell
what Medusa never could?

Women learn
to hate the quick whip
and slither on a path,
or the writhing roomful
in a dream.

Learn beauty
is power, its blossoms
pearling the pane
and the whole sky
trembling with flowers.

Candy

You agreed to be an accomplice,
keep the engine running the night the boy
only a few years older than the rest of us
robbed the pharmacy, entering
with a copy key, sacks of pills
to the car and back, then a final trip
to break the window,
sirens as you rounded the corner.

Only now do we learn
that you loved him.
We didn't even know you were gay,
only reckless, testing your luck, bad heart,
told your whole life to be careful.
To which you handed out quaaludes
like candy, a staggering number
the weekend my parents were away.

Huge party. Friends of friends,
strangers of strangers. I submitted—no,
orchestrated
the despoiling of my flower.
Was it clumsy, hurried, harsh?
Then over and too late to undo.

We are bound together, easier
now that you are dead. Our nights

are bound, your saying yes
and my saying yes, and the dispensing
of pills, the taking of, and a boy,
his body against my body,
and the pharmacy, the siren, love.
Time spins in one direction
then another,
the air sharp with shards,
and your heart
lasting as long as it did.

Foam

I remember foam on every menu
for a season. Hillocks of spit
frilling the plate, brief season
no one clarified, boiled off,
skimmed froth.

Mouthfeel of mushrooms
or beets minus gravity,
whipped into copious foam.

In the fizz of desire, briefly
I was a fountain, endlessly
pouring forth.

Foam is food
if you are starving.

The Classics

Give the victor a slave
if he doesn't have a wife,
a container to be filled. How else
to rid himself of war?

Sometimes it is hard to know—
the ship or the captive
in the hold? Both
called she.

A girl is a series
of openings. A boy,
a collection of limbs.

Nineteen, or fifteen,
the prettiest
among the hoard—
the hero gets
first pick.

My mother was never thin
until she was dying.
The dying diet.

A furtive meal
of bread and figs
after the men

have gone off
to sharpen their swords.

Save yourself
for yourself.
Did my mother
teach me this?
Not in so many words.

Single

Sheila, your name is more telling
of age than your photo.
West Hollywood studio, ours
for two weeks though my husband
will soon leave to decide
what he wants from his life.
Romance or irony?
the mountain of pillows on the bed,
most of them velvet,
and the brass shepherd wrapping
the stem of a table lamp,
a chinoiserie sideboard,
much in powder pink,
tufted bar stools,
so many match boxes
from the Chateau Marmont.
Renting out your jewel box all summer
to travel the capitals of Europe,
you're doing fine. Are you sorry
you never settled for less
than Bogart or Grant?
The message on your door—
May you have the courage—
tears a corner off the gilded cover.
If you were here, we would talk
of love—your choices,
my choices. You've left

us a bottle of champagne
and two flutes so jewel-encrusted
they're impossible to use.
A water glass is fine
for solitary drinking.
Paper roses on the breakfast table
and a basket of goodies, a note
to help ourselves. Gracious Sheila,
I imagine your life is mine.

Casual

Even what isn't fine is fine—
how you make me feel
when you run your hands
over me, when you enter
and we hold still
for a minute and cling
as though we were
each other's long-lost
before rocking our bodies together.

We will never fall madly in love,
marry and have children,
and raise them in the warmth of our love
and be pleased so many years later
that our passion persists.
I may not see you again
for months.

I am feeding regret
into the shredder,
pulling each sheet off the tall stack
and guiding it through.
Though still a little afraid
to say out loud
joy, joy, joy.

I'm Gorgeous Inside

I can afford to live in Laurel Canyon
for a week, rented studio,
can pretend I'm a regular,
know by name the old guys
whiling away the morning with their coffees.
This could be Peoria, Dubuque,
only they're boho rich and maybe famous
from the canyon's glory days of rock and roll.
Back up the hill with my latte,
I'm Gorgeous Inside
affixed to the For Sale sign
on a yellow house, pretty enough
but not drop dead for the three
or is it five million asking?

I want to come home to die
I half joke over drinks with my friends,
hometown I left at seventeen
against the brutality of beauty.
This time I really mean it,
come home at last and let the waning
years of my gorgeous commence.

Five

The Last Summer

Every language has its word for *pussy,*
what passes between boys
before one after the other
takes the dare and throws himself
off the cliff, one frogging his legs
and lifting his arms in triumph
as he falls to the sea.
The local liquor arrives clear
then clouds with ice.
We put down our glasses to watch.
Now the boys are scrambling
back to the top of the cliff
and someone has the idea
to add a somersault
so boy after boy
tumbles through space.
There is no future on the island.
Maybe this is their last summer together
before each goes his own way.
Our ice is already starting to melt.

Sex and Death

I was having sex when my mother died
four hundred miles away.
Why am I telling you this?
Am I so desperate
for attention I will offer up
any part of private to get it?
It seems so.

I've heard orgasm helps
a woman conceive.
I hope I came into being
with a shudder of pleasure.
Little death that ushers life.
Little bliss when the mind goes blank.

When the finish came,
did my mother
alone in her bed cry out?

I don't miss her
anymore, though each time
she visits is a sweet surprise,
like taking off a wig in a dream
and a full head of hair tumbles out,
and blond!

Ode on a Dressing Room in Rome

Poet whose name was writ in water,
tomorrow we'll climb the stairs,
tour his last abode, the narrow bed,
the ceiling painted blue
so he lay on a hillside seeing sky
as death arrived at twenty-five.
But tonight, O deep awkward
in the dress shop, the nice sales girl—
she helped me imagine myself
in swirling patterns of ocean and air—
replaced by the owner
now assessing size and fit, his friends
keeping him company until closing.
He pulls back the curtain, guiding me
into the changing room.
I strip and slip into a dress
that's going to be snug,
it's made to show,
the blue one with the bow,
the sea-green with a décolletage
another woman would wear
with pleasure, with whimsy—
what my husband says I lack.
That's him, off to the side,
worried, he's seen before
my going through while gone.
I change into, out of,

see myself in the mirror one way
then another, part the curtain.
The owner and his friends look,
look away, continue talking
in a language I don't know.
Shame, thou hast thy music too.

Oil on Wood

I could have had you at eighteen—
that's how much older,
bar table between us, blare
of holiday party, how close
we need to sit to talk.

All of my ages swarm
against the mismatch of time,
they don't care what year it is.
The past is a swaying forest of reeds,
watery walls I pass through.

No, I don't need to finish my drink.
Soon I will learn you are bossy in bed.
Then want to be bossed.
By morning, the sorrow of dressing.
What do we do with our bodies now?

Walking alone to the train,
Macy's wreaths and giant bows,
my own porch light left on.
Slow flood of feeling, then I open
today's calendar page,
drooping tulips, a few fallen blossoms—
oil on wood—and record our night,
making it easy
in some future to find you.

Moral Injury

Grainy feed on the flat-screen—
cloudy sky ten thousand miles away—
and it's hard to tell who is the enemy
and who a child with a stick
or a woman carrying laundry.
Somewhere in a suburb of a suburb,
soldiers who once were gamers
playing long past bedtime
now follow the enemy
for days, watch him eating dinner
or kicking a ball with the kids before dark.
The button pushed, the target hit,
high fives all around,
then wander down the hall for a soda.
Soon it is time for lunch.

Shift over, the soldier pulls
into his yard where a clothesline
drags low under the weight of blankets.
The buckeye is thick with butterflies.
An upward shower as they alight
then the sky explodes
with blinking scraps of gold.

The Sea Cure

I steer us into the last spot,
beach parking lot, Tuesday afternoon,
the old and infirm watching
the sea from their cars.
Next to us, the driver lights a bong,
billows of smoke—
contact high, you smirk, stoned
every day for years before illness
took that as well from you.
To the other side, a man sprinkles bird seed
up to his elbow and three pigeons
perch on his arm.
You ask if I'm going to write
about this. I guess the answer is yes
though I'm not yet sure what to say.
You want to die
the way your aunt did,
clamping a hose to the tail pipe
and threading it through the window.
These weekly sessions,
all of us here for the cure,
though there *is* no cure,
only the amplitude of wave
over wave like a hand
smoothing a brow,
letting us rest.

Furnace

Workers load the body
onto the body lift, having first placed it
in pine or plywood, or cardboard,
then use the long-handled tool—
a little like a pizza peel—to slip
the box into the retort already inching
toward two thousand degrees.
It didn't occur to me to watch
though it turns out they let you.
All I saw was the waiting room,
then the office where on my side
of the wide desk on a random block
zoned for light industry
I discussed the cost
and urn options with the sales rep
or maybe the owner, then signed off,
gave my father this.
Reform before the stroke,
he never forgave God after.
Is that why he chose fire?
After, I marvel at how heavy
when handed the box,
mine now to open
or bury or save.

State U

One classmate, old,
thirty or twenty-seven,
had been to war.
The war was over—intermission
between this war and the next.
The teacher asked him for his sources
but he didn't know
there were stairs, that the library started
on the second floor. He'd wandered
the lobby level, couldn't understand
where the books were.
What a thing to admit. Now
he is starting to cry.
The war still ringing in his ears
and exploding behind his eyes.

Soldier, though I do not know
if you are still alive,
let me say that I honor
the wet flag of your shame
spread before us, flag you did not
want to spread but could not hide.
Without permission I have used you,
many times, to stand closer to myself.
Should I thank you for this?

Beached

A whale has washed to shore,
its great muscled body jellying
under the slow push and pull of waves,
its billow of ribs like broken columns,
a cathedral coming off in chunks.

Soon it will be bulldozed
to landfill—junked autos,
rusted slabs, mattress coils piled on top.
Or boats in the night, high tide,
will tow the body back to sea.

We've paid to watch whales breach,
mesmerized by the miraculous
hoist and slap, a hundred tons,
and we, mere subjects in our smallness.
Now we're a ragged circle
outside the caution tape,
more of us coming to see.

The Language of Flowers

The white lily speaks of pure love
but I prefer the cryptic canterbury bell:
"Your letter received."
And from another blue,
the cornflower's "Be gentle with me."
The magnolia's waxy leaves
and first pink-white blossoms
startle the walker in winter:
"I am learning to live without you."

Sometimes sitting in traffic,
not even a daisy on the dashboard,
I find my way
to kind regard.
Or it to me.

One rush hour,
going nowhere,
a visitation of joy.
Stirring scent.
Then gone, the thought
that ushered it.

If Animals Came in Blue

Constrained to a narrow, still
we can't enlarge
ourselves on demand,

our stern invisibles
telling us how much
and no more

to want. Years pass.
Then we're taken
by surprise, and all at once —

that's how it feels — though what
slow plowing of the dark
before the final push to light?

Suddenly in every room
I want you and us.
And in every chair

in every room, in the velvets
by the window,
morning sun on their pelts —

they look like animals,
if animals came in blue —
and on the love seat,

tossing off the piled books.
All morning we've poured
our hearts out.

The body inside the body
is fluid and bangs
against the walls of its container.

Acknowledgments

Thank you to the following publications in which poems from this collection first appeared:

Bayou: "The Wolf Indicator"

Catamaran: "Beggar," "Food is Not Medicine"

Crosswinds: "If Animals Came in Blue"

Cutthroat: "Elsewhere"

Driftwood: "County"

Interlitq: "Method," "Ode on a Dressing Room in Rome," "State U"

Main Street Rag: "Left at the Ruin"

New Millennium: "Moral Injury"

New Ohio Review: "Not the Wolf but the Dog"

Nomadic Coffee: "Blade"

Quartet Journal: "The Feeling of Will-Be-Over"

Radar: "The Door of Mercy"

Rattle: "Women with Men"

River Styx: "Conjoined"

RockPaperPoem: "Forecast"

Tar River Poetry: "The Classics," "Rosy Fingered Dawn"

The Halcyon: "Bitter"

Trampoline: "I Wake at 2 AM to a Girl"

"First Kiss" was published in *A Constellation of Kisses*, ed. Diane Lockward (Terrapin Books, 2019).

The owners of Nomadic Coffee in Oakland, California, invited poet D.A. Powell to select a poem to put in their coffee bags, and he chose the poem "Blade."

Thank you to my brilliant poet friends who offered their good advice about the making of these poems and about making a life of poetry: Melody Lacina, Laura Horn, Betsy Kassoff, Joan Gelfand, Sharon Fain, Katherine Lieban, Susan Dambroff, Susan Cohen, Francesca Bell, Gail Newman, Dawn McGuire, Rebecca Foust, Jeanne Wagner, Lucille Lang Day, Barbara Quick.

Thank you to Elaina Ellis for such full seeing and close reading of the manuscript.

Thank you, most of all, to my beloved husband, Jeffrey Erickson, who inspires me to trust what two people bound by love can make of a shared life.

And to the memory of my parents, Sylvia and Sheldon, whose presence I still feel.

About the Author

Jacqueline Berger is the author of four previous books of poetry, including *The Day You Miss Your Exit* (Broadstone Books, 2018); *The Gift That Arrives Broken* (Autumn House Press, 2010), winner of the Autumn House Poetry Prize; *Things That Burn* (University of Utah Press, 2005), winner of the Agha Shahid Ali Prize in Poetry; and *The Mythologies of Danger* (Bluestem Press, 1997), winner of the Bluestem Award and the Bay Area Book Awards Poetry Prize). Several of her poems have been featured on Garrison Keillor's *Writers Almanac*. She is a professor emerita at Notre Dame de Namur University in Belmont, California, and has recently relocated from San Francisco to the California Central Coast with her husband.